Fear Not!

Angels Are
Waiting to Serve!

Reverend Mike Wanner

Free Kindles
"Healing Presents" Tab

http://www.AngelRaphaelSpeaks.com

Table of Contents

s

Preface

When I was a child, my father got sick with Cancer. He had a hard time, and eventually, God took him, and I missed him. That was many years ago, and I wished that I could have done more for him.

I did not understand, but I wanted to, and it was impossible to know what to do to help others. I tried to comprehend but could not find answers.

Wanting to understand has influenced my life. The one thing that I remembered so firmly was the importance of Kindness.

So, my priorities in life have been Kindness and understanding.

1 - Introduction

In losing my father, I lost my foundation and support system. Everything was scary, fear-filled days were the standard, and for a long time, I did not know how to handle it.

I have felt lost many times along my life journey. Pursuing understanding has been a long and tiring journey for me, but I have had successes and am still in the pursuit of more.

I reached a position of peaceful observation with myself and all that is. In some ways, I was blessed but frequently did not understand how or why.

We humans exist in the physical world, and that can make everything confusing and stressful. The stress of urban living can make it difficult to see all the blessings that are divinely available to us all.

When things happen that we do not understand, our ability to use or avoid them is minimal. The most sophisticated new tool would lack use if we did not know how it should be used.

I offer my experiences and wisdom for your consideration and study in the hope that it will help in your healing and growth.

2 - Has Fear Attacked Your Peace

When fear shows up, I recommend that those impacted take some time right away to transfer their feelings to paper while intending that the procedure takes the negative energy along for the ride.

The procedure, in a way, acknowledges the fear ever so briefly as it moves it away from them. Draining the fear's intensity allows the writer to see themselves taking action to be in charge of the situation.

Like a blood clot in the body, the buildup of fear can cause a dangerous vulnerability. Being able to think clearly and deliberately is a giant step forward in taking care of oneself during the initial realization of the situation.

Fear Shows Up Unexpectedly

Fear is a common challenge amongst all the people in the communities and nations of the world. It can show up everywhere, and it can run from moderately inconvenient to traumatic.

Fear is an inside job when one or many events happen that bring you awareness to something that seems overwhelmingly dangerous or imminently threatening. The realization of fear without proactive resistance can trigger responses within a

6

person that associates memories of similar experiences, that can make the threat seem even more significant.

The fear itself can be like a disease because the impact can severely impact a person's ability to think clearly and react appropriately. There can be a paralysis-like effect when the one in fear, does nothing to prevent doing the wrong thing.

When the one impacted is unable or unwilling to take action to eliminate the problem, complications could result.

The person may lack the knowledge that would be needed to fix the issue and may need advice and help.

The nest step forward to move out of fear is to access the available resources from the physical and spiritual worlds.

Journaling may be helpful to release anxiety by transferring the images in one's head to paper, so relief from stress is started quickly.

Who Can Help You Evaluate?

Please don't let your struggles pile up on top of each other with no hope in sight and continue to push you down.

Step 1. Decide if you like the situation enough to stay put or whether you would like to choose to initiate change.

Step 2. If you want to change things, decide if you have options readily available where you can take control of the situation.

Step 3. If the answer to step 2 is no, decide if you have people who might help:

> Mother
> Father
> Sister
> Brother
> Aunt
> Uncle
> Cousins
> Boyfriend
> Girlfriend
> Best friend
> In-Laws
> Boss
> Co-workers

Is Counseling or Advisors Available?

Do You Belong to a Company, Community, or Service Organization that could Offer Guidance?

Many businesses, service organizations, and Church or Spiritual groups offer levels of counseling for a variety of challenges that their members or employees might experience.

Counseling services can frequently offer an outside perspective and maybe the right place to start sorting through the crisis and all the challenges around it.

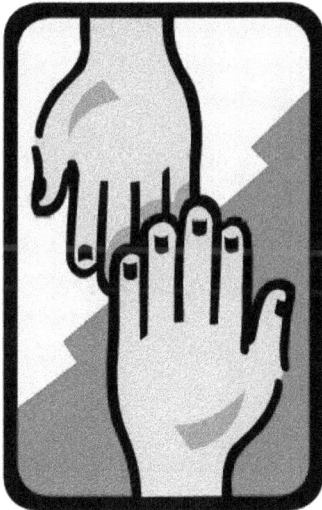

Counseling Services

Medical & Spiritual Checkups Plus

It may seem strange for a minister writing about Angels to be suggesting so many options that are not Angelic connections. The reality is that you are a physical person living in the physical world, and people typically need four different types of support for the most optimal life.

Physical Support

Your Medical Doctor may be more familiar with you than most other people, and you know his or her objectivity and value as a consultant.

Emotional Support

Family and friends can provide invaluable, understanding, and loving support when you need it most.

Mental Support

People with ongoing psychological support from a professional may be wise to check in for advice. People not with a psychiatric practitioner may need one if their Medical Doctor suggests it for this intense challenge.

Spiritual Support

Minister, Rabbis, and Priests in your faith tradition can provide continuity within your belief systems that can help you subtly maintain your peace and power perspective.

3 - Your Comfort Zone

Every fear that comes up can be different from each concern you have ever had previously. While you are getting ready to decide on a path forward, you can tune into your internal comfort level.

Like medicine affects a diagnosis, attitude, and comfort level or zone impacts on the success that is produced by actions taken. I started above with direct options so you could start the selection process and build up some confidence in your decisiveness as you narrow the field of possibilities needed.

It may be that chapter two has enough ideas to implement so that you can get moving in the right direction and if that works, Hooray. When the fear is eliminated, and you are again at peace, you will have done enough to survive the fear's grip.

It may be that connecting with Angels is outside your comfort zone, and you do not wish to do it. You, of course, have free will, so there is no requirement for you to do that.

From my perspective, the most crucial component is for you to choose a focus that eliminates fear. You are familiar that in your car and your house, there can be radios or TVs that have very intense events playing that can be dynamically changed with the selection of a different channel.

The fear vibrations triggered similarly within your body can be equally shifted by the mental change of your focus from fear to something more joyful. It is helpful to know what brings fear to your mind and also what turns it off.

As you become more mindful, you acquire the opportunity to control more of your body in ways that can make even more enhancements to your health. The "gold standard" of personal peace is the attainment of "Homeostasis" where the body is in optimal alignment physically, emotionally, mentally, and spiritually so that your internal healing system is optimized.

Each human is unique, and personal awareness and comfort within your skin allow optimization of each facet of the life force you were given and the way you can use it in the days ahead.

There is a pandemic in the world right now, and that adds to the ordinary plague of doubt, fear, personal insignificance, judgment, powerlessness, depression, addictions, incompetence, and despair. Most, if not all, of us have used some crutches or excuses in our lives.

Each morning brings new opportunities to recreate your life and become a shining star example of rebirth and Phoenix Symbology. Please consider the daily chance to optimize your experience and future.

Please ask for any help you need. Deciding to ask for help from within your community or the Divine one is a giant action step in the right direction.

4 - Don't Know About Angels? - It's OK

It could be that your spiritual tradition does not teach about Angels. I invite you to work within your spiritual beliefs and connectivity to encourage spiritual support that aligns with your religious tradition.

Asking for help is the action needed while connecting with the hierarchy of the Divine. The next step after asking is listening for the queues that will take you further down the perfect path for your journey.

I share my experience and invite you to share yours so others who were taught like you can build upon your involvement in their lives.

As a Vietnam Veteran seeking personal healing, I was on an experiential journey that took me to Spiritual Healing and Reiki. Originating in Japan, Reiki was a natural healing system similar to the "laying on of hands" that was discussed in the bible.

While practicing Reiki on myself and others, I learned about a course that had the subtitle "Healing With The Energy of Angels." I took the course and learned about Angels and have not looked back since.

Integrated Energy Therapy (IET) is a healing modality that uses an Angelic Heartlink to simplify the understanding and connection to Angels. Embracing and understanding the possibilities allows practitioners and their clients to focus on intention expediently so that angelic alignment can be experienced and used without fear and doubt.

The first blessing of working with IET is the ability to help with releasing stuffed emotions and cellular memory. I still find it amazing how clients make so much progress so fast when they are ready to heal and release doubts about their significance in the Divine Order.

IET was proposed initially to those in the healing community who had practices offering modalities to the general public, and that worked well and helped a lot of people

IET through Master Instructors. Like me, now offer classes for the general public, and one that might help people with fear is called "Healing Angels of the Energy Field."

While classes like that are comprehensive, getting help from the Angels can be started on your own without any cost whatsoever.

5 - Angels Can Help You Claim Your Power

There is a lot that humans do that they know is not healthy for them, but they do it anyhow. If that is true for you, then you may want to revisit those aspects of your lifestyle and restructure your activities with a fresh perspective.

After a career in Emergency Medical Services and a calling to ministry, I have seen a lot of people make changes, amaze their doctors and families and friends, and create new repurposed futures for themselves.

When many people hear something upsetting, they can drop down into a fear-based reaction that does not serve them well or help them function. Calling on the Angels can help people take charge of their lives.

You are already started if you are on the progressive path that I suggested in Chapter 2. With that work done, you are ready to look into the possibilities that Angels may be able to offer you.

I write a lot and have many things to share, but I am also still a student and do my evaluations of things that others suggest to me. I keep asking God and the Angels for Guidance, so I pay attention to the messages that I need to process.

Please feel free to send me your comments and suggestions so that I can ask On-High, listen, and communicate more to you and others later.

I want to pique your interest in steps that empower you to stifle anything that might slow down your Soul Purpose or impede the choices that you make that could help others.

When your internal Guidance reacts to an idea, concept, or Angel's name, please consider learning more, while opening your discernment wide. Please see pain and problems as invitations to visit reality as a topic needing study, which may well be beneficial to others.

One of the best things that we all can do is reach out to uplift others. God will see that, and you might just be able to optimize their life and yours at the same time.

Please consider each new idea as a resolution to your problem or a step on the path that will.

Here are some ideas about understanding Angels better:

1. Angels Are always around us waiting to be called.
2. You can speak to the Angels naturally like people, or in Prayer, or your mind.
3. Angels need to be invited before they can work on your behalf.
4. Angels are team players – Invite One Angel, and you have multiple supporters right away.
5. Angel work is in the spiritual realm; You won't see them doing real things, but they will work within their world and ability.

6 - Connecting With Angels

I am pleased to introduce you first to Archangel Michael.-
The Archangel of Safety and Protection. Michael is frequently
pictured as God's Defender of the people.

While Michael is part of the angel team, many people report that uttering his name triggers the protection, safety, energy, light, or strength they need to protect them from the darkness they face. I invite you now to settle down and take a few deep breaths and invite him into your awareness.

The Invitation could be a simple everyday language statement, a prayer, or merely a thought. I sometimes thank God for the Angels before I talk to them.

If you have fear at this moment, there would be no better time to start a dialogue with Angel Michael. Please allow yourself to be free in the conversation that goes on in your mind. Please pause and do it now, so you have your first experience and then can build upon that.

Angels are user friendly and inviting them is as simple as any conversation. I recommend that you develop a relationship over time to simplify your ability to become comfortable with a special Angel or group of them.

Michael can be referred to as an Angel or Archangel by different people with different Spiritual upbringings. Both terms are equally acceptable, and Archangel indicates a level of seniority.

It is good to note the different experiences you have with each Angel so that your notes remind you of your success at connecting at such a level with Divine energy.

Archangel Raphael - The Angel of Healing

I am pleased to introduce you next to Archangel Raphael - The Archangel of Healing. Raphael is frequently pictured with the phrase "Take Courage!: God Has Healing In-store for You."

While Raphael is part of the angel team, many people report that uttering his name triggers the healing, connectivity, guilt release, and innocence they need to feel empowered. I invite you now to settle down and take a few deep breaths and invite him into your awareness.

The Invitation could be a simple everyday language statement, a prayer, or merely a thought. I sometimes thank God for the Angels before I talk to them.

If you need healing, guilt release, or Divine Reconnection at this moment, there would be no better time to start a dialogue with Angel Raphael. Please allow yourself to stop unwanted chatter in your mind. Please pause and do it now, so you have one more Angel connection experience upon which you can have as experience.

Angels are user friendly and inviting them is as simple as any conversation. I recommend that you develop a relationship over time to simplify your ability to become comfortable with a special Angel or group of them.

Raphael can be referred to as an Angel or Archangel by different people with different Spiritual upbringings. Both terms are equally acceptable, and Archangel indicates a level of seniority.

It is good to note the different experiences you have with each Angel so that your notes remind you of your success at connecting at such a high level with Divine energy.

Choosing An Angel

You may have Guidance, and you would do well to follow it. If You do Not Have a clue where to start, Try This Process.

Write a short paragraph about your concerns so you can transfer the emotional connection into words and allow yourself some balance and a break. Please write below what bothers you most without thinking too deeply. Spontaneous writing helps clarity.

_____

_____

_____

_____

_____

I have developed the following process because, with it, I can picture a grid in my head that shows me where people need energy work most.

If you do this, you can use the values to choose an Angel to invite who is most likely the right choice for the issues that are challenging you.

Please make this a low-stress exercise by remembering when you invite an angel, s/he brings the whole team connectivity with them, so everybody is available to help.

So, You choose your concerns, take the test, pick an Angel, invite the Angel you selected, and allow your life to optimize more.

Take The Emotional Intensity Test

ReverendMikeWanner@aol.com

Rate the strength of the Following Emotions on a scale from
One (Least) to Ten (Most).

Emotion	How Do You Feel?
Guilt	_____
Distrust	_____
Shame	_____
Threat	_____
Overly - Responsible	_____
Heartache	_____
Betrayal	_____
Resentment	_____
Anger	_____
Stress	_____
Powerlessness	_____
Fear	_____

Match Your Emotional Intensity to an Angel

No Worries. They All Work Together Always.
{You Can't Go Wrong}

Emotion	Angel
Guilt	Raphael (& More Angels)
Distrust	Gabriel (& More Angels)
Shame	Celestina (& More Angels)
Threat	Celestina (& More Angels)
Overly – Responsible	Faith (& More Angels)
Heartache	Cassiel (& More Angels)
Betrayal	Cassiel (& More Angels)
Resentment	Daniel (& More Angels)
Anger	Daniel (& More Angels)
Stress	Sarah (& More Angels)
Powerlessness	Sarah (& More Angels)
Fear	Michael (& More Angels)

Invitation Suggestion

Angels Are Always Around Us

They Respect Our Free Will

If We Want Their Help – We Must Ask!

If we ask, they will Surround Us, Protect Us,
Guide Us, and Direct Us

Declare Who You Want to Connect With and Your Request

Use Your Own Words, or at least the following.

I Invite Angel

{If Not Sure – Choose Angel Raphael – The Angel Of Healing}

I Request Your Support With

Thank You

7 - Wrap Up

Working with the Angels is not a quick seminar or book; it is a journey that will take some time. You can move at your speed and adjust the effort to fit within your life in a way that is both helpful and comfortable.

In my experience, the efforts expended are worth the time investment. I purposely limited the content offered above because there is no need to overwhelm you with information.

Archangel Michael or Archangel Raphael are each significant enough to convince you of the power available to help you. If you are open spiritually to blessings, I invite you to connect with either of them or any of the other Angels mentioned.

The Angels changed my life, and I believe they can change yours. I pray that you accept the Invitation from me and invite the Angels into your life.

Angels Can fly because they take themselves lightly.
That's A Good Example For Us.
Smile to share God's Light.

More Information About Angels
https://AngelRaphaelSpeaks.com
https://www.LearnIET.com or
E-mail: ReverendMikeWanner@aol.com

For
Considering
These
Ideas

9 - Angels Please Prayers - Addiction Help

Addict's

Angels of Healing Selected
Help Me to Stay Directed
Come To Me From The Sky
I Am Ready to Succeed Not Try
If I Don't Invite You In
I Might Not Win
I Have Been Lost For Too Long
Help Me To Stay Strong

Alcoholic's

Angels of Healing On High
Help Me to Stay Dry
Come To Me From The Sky
I Am Ready to Succeed Not Try
If I Don't Invite You In
I Might Not Win
I Have Been Lost For Too Long
Help Me To Stay Strong

Prayers From

ANGELS ARE ALWAYS
AROUND ADDICTS
AND ALCOHOLICS

HELP IS NEAR NOW!
INVITE IT IN!

REVEREND
MIKE WANNER

http://AngelRaphaelSpeaks.com/AAAAAAA/
The Link Above Has the Core Messages from the book on drop-down pages.

10 - On-Line Prayer Request Links

Circle Of Miracles
https://circleofmiracles.org/services/prayer-request/

The Center Of Being, Inc.
(Integrated Energy Therapy)
https://www.learniet.com/angel-ariel/need-angelic-support/

The Theosophical Society Order of Service Free Healing Network:

1. For People http://www.theoservice.org/special/names-by-email.shtml

2. For Animals https://www.theoservice.org/spec.../animal-healing-names.shtml

Prayer Writing Resource

http://Create-A-Prayer.com

11 - Books Category Resources
at www.Amazon.com

Distant Healing (or Mail List) e-mail mikewann@voicenet.com

Veterans Healing Six Pack plus 2
http://angelraphaelspeaks.com/healing-books/veterans/

PTSD Power Pack
http://angelraphaelspeaks.com/healing-books/ptsd/

Angel Raphael Speaks Series & Other Angel Books
http://angelraphaelspeaks.com/

Reiki
http://angelraphaelspeaks.com/healing-books/reiki/

Children
http://angelraphaelspeaks.com/healing-books/children/

Emergency Medical Kindness
http://angelraphaelspeaks.com/healing-books/emergency-medical-kindness/

Cancer
http://angelraphaelspeaks.com/healing-books/cancer/

Addictions
http://angelraphaelspeaks.com/healing-books/addictions/

Miscellaneous Healing
http://angelraphaelspeaks.com/healing-books/misc-healing/

Prison Books - 60+ Prison Books
http://angelraphaelspeaks.com/prison-books/

12 - Private Channeling

Angel Raphael Speaks, a series of messages channeled through Reverend Mike Wanner for the Highest good and Highest Healing of all concerned.

Many questions arise about Reverend Mike doing private channeling, and he does help with that, so E-mail him.

Reverend Mike is available worldwide as a psychic channel, emotional release facilitator, spiritual energy practitioner, teacher, and public speaker.

He looks forward to meeting you soon! E-mail - mikewann@voicenet.com 215-342-1270

PRIVATE SPIRITUAL READINGS/channelings or Spiritual Healing Sessions can be by telephone or in-person.

Rev. Mike is available for individual, intuitive one-on-one sessions with you, his Guide Family, and your Guides. He helps by offering clarity on emotional situations about your life, your purpose, your spirituality, and your release of stuffed emotions and cellular memory.

Connect to the love of your Guides today!

For more information, please visit
http://angelraphaelspeaks.com/channel/

13 - Reverend Mike Wanner

Rev. Mike Wanner started his spiritual and ministerial studies with Reiki in 1993 and had studied seven styles of Reiki in the U.S., Japan, Canada, Denmark, and Australia. He is certified to teach.

He became certified to teach Integrated Energy Therapy® in 1999 and co-taught the first IET class of the new millennium. Mike began dowsing in 2001.

Ordained as an Interfaith Minister of the Circle of Miracles Ministry and a Metaphysical Minister of the International Metaphysical Ministry, Rev. Mike practices and teaches spiritual energy therapies in the Philadelphia Area.

He was a faculty member of the Medical Mission Sister's Center for Human Integration's School of Integrated Body/Mind Therapies in Fox Chase, Philadelphia, PA, for twelve years.

For a complete Biography, please visit
http://ReverendMikeWanner.com/Bio

www.ingramcontent.com/pod-product-compliance
Lightning Source LLC
Chambersburg PA
CBHW060600030426
42337CB00019B/3580